THE ĀSURĪ-KALPA, A WITCHCRAFT PRACTICE OF THE ATHARVA-VEDA

I.—INTRODUCTION.

The ritual literature of the Atharva-Veda, like that of the other Vedas, has attached to itself certain pariçistas, or supplements Of these, the thirty-fifth, according to the best accessible MS, is the Āsurī-Kalpa, an abhicāra, or witchcraft practice, containing rites to be used in connection with the āsurī-plant The question as to what this plant was will be discussed below The use of the word *kalpa* for such a text is explained by a passage in the Atharvanīya-Paddhati, which states, on the authority of Uparvarsa,[1] that in addition to the five AV *kalpas*—Kāuçika, Vāitāna, Naksatra, Çānti, and Āñgirasa—which are called *çruti* 'inspired,' there are certain other kalpas which are to be considered as *smrti* 'handed down by tradition '[2]

Three MSS have been consulted in preparing this paper. Two of them are copies of the pariçistas of the AV , the third is a commentary to the Āsurī-Kalpa. All three are loans to Dr. Bloomfield from the British Government in India. Just here I may say that I am greatly indebted to Dr. Bloomfield for the use of these MSS, for the encouragement and assistance which he has given me, and for his kindness in looking over my work. The MSS are as follows

A, large sheets of light yellow paper, bound in book form, written lengthwise in a large clear hand and with considerable care It is a modern copy

B, narrow sheets of light blue paper, bound in book form, written lengthwise, text fuller in places than the preceding, but in a poor hand and with numerous errors It must be a very recent copy Both of these MSS are numbered 23

S (Scholiast), much older than either of the preceding, single sheets of light brown paper grown dark at the edges, written lengthwise as the other MSS, but in a very poor, though large,

[1] A mīmānsā (pūrva-) teacher See Life and Essays of H T Colebrooke, Vol II, pp 319–49

[2] Cf J A O S XI 377, Bloomfield, On the Position of the Vāitāna-Sūtra in the Literature of the Atharva-Veda

hand It contains three sections or chapters *Part first* (folios 1b–6a[7]) contains all the practices in brief form, and occupies about one-fourth of the MS *Part second* (folios 6a[7]–7b[6]) treats only of the externals of the principal rite, and occupies scarcely one-tenth of the MS *Part third* is an elaborate commentary on what has preceded, but in its present condition deals with only about two-thirds of the practices, since the MS lacks some folios at the close [1] This MS is numbered 120, but is also marked *p* (*pathāni*) *18, sam* (*samvat*) *1880–81*, and, on the last folio, written across the end on the margin, *347* From the appearance of the MS it might be as old as one hundred and fifty years, and since *sam 1880–81* probably has reference to Kielhorn's Report,[2] the MS may be as old as it looks It contains about 200 çlokas

At the beginning of *part third* it names Mahādeva as the speaker,[3] who introduces his commentary (see p 11, note 19) by saying 'It [the mantra] is not to be uttered (performed) without teachers, by the precept of a teacher this magic power (success) [comes into being] Accordingly in a single final commentary the Āsurī-[rite] should succeed,'—

vinā guruṇ akartavyam guruvākyena siddhīdam[4] (cod *sīdhī-*),
ekāntimatīkāmadhye (cod *ekānte-*) *sādhayeta tad āsurī* 2

Mahādeva[5] is spoken of as the seer of the divine āsurī-text,[6] and as becomes a ṛṣi he speaks of the Gāyatrī, Triṣṭubh, and Anuṣṭubh metres (*gayatrītriṣṭubanuṣṭupchandaḥ*), after which he proceeds to give full instructions concerning the rites

[1] *Part first* seems to be in fact a version of the pariçiṣṭa, fuller than the text and differing from it in some passages, but still essentially the same The chief points of difference have been noted as readings of *S* They have been put into çloka form where the MS seemed to warrant it Readings from *parts second* and *third* are so marked

[2] See p 5, foot-note 1 The MS is catalogued on p 58

[3] The pariçiṣṭas as a whole are in the form of dialogues Cf Weber, History of Indian Literature, p 153

[4] The conjectural reading *siddhīdam* requires a regular fem noun to be regarded as neu, but for this text it may be allowable, since the MS departs widely in places from all rules of grammar, and also treats *siddhi* as a neu in other passages

The comma and period (, and) have been used in all Sanskrit passages as the simplest means of transliterating the two Sanskrit marks of punctuation (| and ||)

[5] An epithet of Rudra or Çiva, also of Viṣṇu and the name of various persons It is an appropriate title, "Great-Lord," for the teacher of such a text

[6] *asya çryāsurīmantrasya* (cod *çrīasu*) *mahādeva ṛṣiḥ*

Apart from its subject-matter ***S*** possesses no little interest, because it contains abundant evidence of the character of the people having to do with its rites. It is exceedingly corrupt, as a few examples may suffice to show. The common writing for *sapta* is *satpa*, for *āsurī*, *asuri*, for *sūksma*, *suksma*, for *cūrna*, *curna*, etc *juhiyat* and *jūhīyāta* are used for *juhuyāt*, *mryate* for *mriyate*, etc: *rdayam* is found for *hrdayam*, *bhimantritena* for *abhi-* (beginning of a sentence), *karaye* for *-yet*, *titha* for *tithir*, etc little or no attention is paid to saṁdhi the confusion of sibilants,[1] *s* for *ç* and vice versa, is exceedingly common and other curious freaks in spelling occur, notably the use of *cy* for *c* (*cyurna* for *cūrṇa*, and *muncyati* for *muñcati*), which is of some interest from a phonetic standpoint, and the writing of the word *vaçīkaratukāma* in eight different ways, while using it but twelve times, with a mistake of some kind in every single instance.[2] The errors are doubtless due in part to later copyists, but, from the present state of corruption, it may be safe to infer that the original MS was bad at the start, for it seems hardly possible that the scribes should be guilty of all the errors which it contains, even if the present MS is the result of several successive transcriptions The nature of the mistakes stamps the writer at once as an ignorant and perhaps degraded person It is about such a document as might be expected to be written in English by some Voodoo doctor among the blacks of the South. Numerous repetitions serve to light up otherwise hopeless passages, and when the brief outlines of the pariçista are combined with the commentary the whole practice becomes clear. No two of the MSS exactly agree in the order in which the different forms of the rite are treated, and ***B*** has a passage not found in either ***A*** or ***S*** Fortunately the pariçista is mostly written in çlokas, which is of great service in determining the true reading[3] In style the pariçista is somewhat like the sūtras, being terse and technical in its forms of expression, and consisting mostly of what may

[1] Cf PROC A O S, May, 1886 Introduction to the Study of the Old-Indian Sibilants, by Prof Bloomfield and Dr Edward H Spieker.

[2] It may be said in addition that there is hardly a sentence in the entire MS in which there are not mistakes in the case-forms, the most common being the use of a stem-form for an acc

[3] In the text, where a MS reading is of no importance, it has been thought best to omit it, so, in the quotations from ***S*** the MS reading has been omitted where the emendation is obvious, where the same mistake is repeated several times, and, in a few instances, where MS evidence warrants the change, on the other hand, where it has been thought best to do so, the passage has been quoted verbatim

be called rules, the commentary is, of course, more like an ordinary text.

In this paper the attempt has been made not only to present a correct version of the pariçiṣṭa, so far as the material at hand would allow, but also to reproduce to some extent the scholiast by citing mostly from the first division, such passages, with the text, as bear on the same part of the rite, and by incorporating into the commentary accompanying the translation such other passages as throw light upon those already cited, or give an idea of additional matters not treated of in the text at all. In this way most of the salient points of *S* have been preserved without, at the same time, copying its tiresome minuteness of detail and unending repetitions—not that the commentary is of so much importance in itself, for, as has been shown, it represents the work of a person of little intelligence apparently, certainly of small acquirements, but that the picture of the whole might be as complete as possible. The practice of witchcraft forms a dark chapter in the history of mankind, and anything that throws light upon the attitude of mind in which its devotees have practiced their curious rites is not to be despised. The "meditations" of *S* may not be without their suggestions to those who care to read between the lines, and the whole practice is a curious bit of evidence of the power of superstition over the human mind.

While the Āsuri-Kalpa has proved a rich field for emendation, and has afforded some opportunity for conjecture, it has not been altogether unfruitful in new material, as the following list will show.

SIMPLE STEMS

Denominative Verb: *piṣṭaya*, to grind up, make into meal.

Nouns (members of compounds): *nastika* [*nasti*], destruction; *ravi*,[1] a tree or plant of some kind; *ṣaḍi* (not in a comp.), a collection of six; *sruca* (?) [*sruc*], sacrifice-ladle.

Adjectives: *pretaka* [*preta*], belonging to a dead [man]. Possibly (?) *jigāṅsa*, desiring to conquer.

Particles: *klīm*, *kṣāum*, and *çrīm*.[2]

Analogical Vocative: *duhite* [*duhitar*], O daughter.

New Meanings or Uses: *sureçvarī* (compound stem), āsurī (plant and probably also goddess). So *lakṣmī*, apparently and possibly *çrī*. *caturtham* (?), fourthly (as adverb).

[1] See page 25, foot-note 4.

[2] Evidently from *çrī* 'beauty, welfare.' These words are used as part of a muttered spell, and have, therefore, no particular meaning.

COMPOUND STEMS

Nouns *aprajatva*, childlessness *utkaraṇa*, overcoming (?)

Adjectives *dakṣiṇakarṇika*, having its point (ear) to the south *devīja*, goddess-born *raktavāsasa*, having a reddish garment *vaçyaga*, subdued Possibly *pratyāmukha*, facing

Neuters as Adverbs *dinatrayam*, at the three parts of the day (A M, M, and P M) *dināṣṭakam*, at the eight parts (watches) of the day. Possibly (?) *saptāhanam*, at the seventh dawn.

COMPOUNDS OF A MORE GENERAL CHARACTER

aparājaya, invincibleness *karmakārikā* (fem. of adj -*raka*), deed-performer. *nāgendra*, a plant, probably Betel *vaçīkartukāma*, the desire to render submissive. Possibly also *surati*, a plant of some kind

A few words have as yet baffled all attempts at a solution They will be mentioned as they occur

That the Āsurī-Kalpa must at one time have occupied a position of some importance appears from the fact that it is mentioned, according to Weber, Ind Stud XIII 415, under the name Āsuriyah Kalpaḥ in the Mahābhāsya IV 1, 19, Vārttikam f 19b In this connection it may be added that the conjecture offered by Professor Bloomfield (J. A O S. XI 378) "*pañcakalpah* is probably not to be understood (with Weber, Ind Stud XIII 455) as one studying five different *kalpas*, i e *çrāuta-sūtras*, but means an Atharvavedin who is familiar with these five *kalpas*," i e. the five belonging to the AV, has recently been confirmed by the discovery, made by the same scholar, of the word *pañcakalpī* (stem -*in*) used in the colophon of a Kāuç MS[1] to mean the writer of a Kāuç. MS In connection with *pañcakalpah*, says Weber (loc cit), the Mahābhāsya (Vartt 3f 67a) mentions the words *kālpasūtrah*, *pārāçarakalpikah*, and *mātrkalpikah*. This last word Weber does not attempt to define, but says of it "Letzteres Wort ist in der vorliegenden Beziehung unklar" In the Kāuçika-Sūtra, 8, 24, is mentioned a gana of hymns (AV. II 2, VI 111, and VIII 6) under the title *mātrnāmāni*, the object of which is the preventing or removing of evil, and Atharva-Pariçista[2] 34, 4, mentions the same gana with the

[1] No 86 Report on the Search for Sanskrit MSS in the Bombay Presidency, 1880–81, by F Kielhorn

[2] *A* No 32, *B* No 34 The latter numbering makes the Āsurī-Kalpa No 37, for each MS gives between it and the Ganamālā two other pariçistas—

addition of AV IV 20, under the same name.[1] It also adds, *iti mātṛgaṇaḥ*. As *kalpasūtraḥ* means one familiar with the Kalpa-Sūtras, and *pārāçarakalpikaḥ* seems to have been used of a person who had studied the Pārāçara-Kalpa,[3] it is safe to infer that the word *mātṛkalpikaḥ* meant one who was familiar with or made use of the Mātṛ-Kalpa, and such a text may yet be found. If it ever appears, Professor Bloomfield conjectures that it will prove to be a ritual for the use of a priest in connection with this Mātṛgaṇa. The presence of these words in the Mahābhāṣya, which contains many Atharvanic words not found elsewhere, cited as they are without explanation, goes to show that they were all well understood by the people of Patañjali's time, and therefore referred to rites and practices so familiar to the Hindoos that the mere name was sufficient to make the reader understand the author's meaning. As they are all Atharvanic, and the word Asurī-Kalpaḥ is also Atharvanic, there can be no doubt that the Āsurī-Kalpaḥ and the Āsurīyaḥ Kalpaḥ are essentially the same, though the text may have suffered some changes at the hands of later authorities on the uses of āsurī, and it is evident that the pariçiṣṭa must have had considerable currency among those who made use of Atharvan rites. Additional evidence of the familiarity of the Hindoos with such practices is to be found in the Laws of Manu (XI 63), where the practice of witchcraft (*abhicāra*) and of magic with roots (*mūlakarman*) is mentioned in a list of secondary crimes (*upapātaka*). This reference also makes clear the fact that such practices are old, for they must have been well established when the Mānava-Dharmaçāstra took its present shape, and go back, therefore, in all probability, some hundreds of years before our era. On the other hand, it must be said that the MSS bear marks of a late origin. *S* mentions the Hindoo trinity (*brahmaviṣṇuhara*), contains the Buddhistical word *hevara*, uses the gen. for the loc. and ins., etc., and all the MSS contain forms (transfers to the *a*-declension, etc.) due to analogy and not cited in any of the dictionaries, besides exhibiting in the subject-matter certain

the Mahābhiṣeka and the Anuloma-Kalpa. *B* does not number the latter or the Āsurī-Kalpa, but has after the Mahābhiṣeka what is evidently a corruption for 35. The PETERS LEX., with *A*, makes the Anuloma-Kalpa No. 34. The numbering of *B* has been taken to correspond to Dr. Bloomfield's edition of the Kāuç.

[1] Cf. Weber, Omina et Portenta, pp. 350–53.

[2] Not in *A* or *B*, but see Bloomfield, Kāuç. S. 24, note 5.

[3] Cf. Weber, Ind. Stud. XIII 445.

tendencies which are recognized as modern. They are mentioned below.

The word *āsurī* is the fem. of an adj. from *asura* "spirit, demon," and therefore means primarily, "belonging to, or having to do with, spirits or demons." Under the form *āsurī*, the PETERS LEX. gives the meaning, schwarzer Senf, Sinapis ramosa Roxb[1] From the evidence of the MSS, *āsurī* must be a plant with a pungent leaf, and must bear fruit (*phala*) and flowers, moreover, a religious meditation (*dhyāna*) of ***S***, which can hardly refer to anything else, speaks of the "bright four-sided granter of wishes", then of the same as "reddish," "blue-colored," "having a sword in the hand," "having a hook in the hand," "having a 'red-stone' in the hand," etc All these expressions are based upon characteristics of the plant, as will appear below. In describing the oblation the pariçista says 'The wise man should make meal of rājikā' (*rājikām piṣṭayed budhaḥ*), while ***S*** in the same passage speaks of āsurī as made into meal The word *rājikā*, in fact, occurs in ***S*** only in **part third**, never in connection with *āsurī*, and always where the latter might be expected The same is true of the word *rājasarṣapa*, for example,—

> *vidhāne pūrvavat karmapratimām rājasarṣapāiḥ,*
> *pūrvavat kārayen nyāsaṁ, chedayet pūrvavad api*

'In [his] preparation, as before, [one should cause] an image for the rite [to be made] with black mustard seeds As in the former case, he should cause the [limb]-placing ceremony to be performed, he should cause [the image] to be chopped also as before' The word *rājikā*, which was left untranslated above, is the common name for the Black Mustard of India This plant has bright yellow flowers, and bears small dark seeds contained in a pod which is tipped by a long, straight, flattened, and seedless beak[2] In all members of the Mustard Family, the pungency pervades the entire plant[3] There can be no doubt that this was the plant actually used, and it is plain that the ignorant and superstitious devotee saw a goddess in the plant itself,[4] and found,

[1] Wm Roxburg, Flora Indica, Semapore, 1832

[2] Hooker Flora of British India, I 157 The Black Mustard of Europe, which is closely related, is described as having smooth erect pods which are somewhat four-sided and tipped with a sword-shaped style They contain small dark brown or nearly black seeds The Black Mustard of the U S is similar

[3] Gray, Introduction to Structural and Systematic Botany, and Vegetable Physiology, 1873, p 389 f

[4] Cf the frequent similar personifications of the AV

perhaps, in the effect of the seeds upon his palate an evidence of her supernatural power[1] The "red-stone" (*rudhira*) mentioned above, and defined by the dictionaries as a certain red stone, not a ruby, here plainly means the seeds in the pod of the āsurī-plant, while the pod itself is probably the "sword," and possibly also the "hook"

The chief object to be attained was the subduing of another to one's will, or the destruction of an enemy The use of the hymns of the AV for the latter purpose is sanctioned by the Laws of Manu (XI 33) 'With the thought 'one should utter (perform) the hymns of the Atharva-Veda,' [let him be] without hesitation, the 'word' is the Brahman s weapon, you know, with it the twice-born should smite [his] enemies,'—

> *çrutīr atharvāñgirasīḥ kuryād ity avicārayan,*
> *vāk çastram vai brāhmanasya tena hanyād arīn dvijah* 33

The other practice, as has been stated, is pronounced criminal by the same authority The rite itself is briefly as follows after certain introductory ceremonies, the person grinds up mustard into meal, with which he makes an image representing the person whom he desires to overcome or destroy Having muttered certain spells to give efficiency to the rite, he chops up the image, anoints it with ghee (melted butter), curds, or some similar substance, and finally burns it in a "sacred-fire-pot" The idea that an image thus destroyed accomplishes the destruction of the person represented, or at least does him serious harm, still survives in India, and it can be duplicated in almost any country in which witchcraft has been practiced The Sāmavidhāna-Brāhmana contains a similar practice, in which an image of dough is roasted so as to cause the moisture to exude, and it is then cut to pieces and eaten by the sorcerer An image of wax has been largely used in various countries, the life of the enemy represented having been supposed to waste away as the wax gradually melted over a slow fire This process was known to the Greeks, to the Romans, to the Germans, and even to the Chaldeans.[2] A vari-

[1] This may also account for the name, since at the time when these practices originated the Hindoos were both very superstitious and extremely unscientific in all matters pertaining to natural phenomena, and they would, therefore, quite naturally assign the pungency of the plant to some spirit or demon

[2] Cf Theocr Idyll II 28, Hor Epod XVII 76, Grimm, Deutsche Mythologie, 1017 ff, Lenormant, Chaldean Magic, p 5, foot-note 1, and p 63, Burnell, Sāmavidhāna-Brāhmana, Vol I, Introd p xxv, and see p 26, foot-note 1, end

ation of the same performance is to fill the image with pins, attach a hated name to it, and set it away to melt or dry up according to the material used. This is said to be still practiced in some parts of America, England and the Continent[1] It is reported that a practice of this kind, i e the making of an effigy to be used for his destruction by means of sorcery, was tried on Henry VI of England, and early in the present century a similar trick was used against the Nizām of the Deccan.[2] Among the Indians of our own country, the Ojibway sorcerers were supposed to be able to transfer a disease from one person to another by a somewhat similar process. They were accustomed to make, for the patient who paid them, a small wooden image representing his enemy, then, piercing the heart of this image, they put in small powders, and pretended by this means, with the help of certain incantations, to accomplish the desired end.[3] The fact that an image has been so universally used in witchcraft practices is no more remarkable than the fact that all nations have made use of images to represent their gods in religious worship, and the two things may both be referred to some law of the human mind by which similar conditions produce similar results There is no discoverable connection between the Ojibway's wooden image and the Hindoo's effigy of dough other than the mere fact that each is the outcome of a desire to injure, and nature teaches them both to think of what is practically the same expedient

The minor practices of the Āsurī-Kalpa, which are designed either to work harm to an enemy or good to the practitioner, will be found in their turn below. They seem to indicate a desire on the part of the author to furnish a short cut to power and to some of the more important blessings which were supposed to be gained by the sacrifices prescribed by the Brāhmanas, indeed, the practices of the Āsurī-Kalpa, as a whole, seem to show a disposition to supplant certain religious forms by simpler magical rites, while endeavoring at the same time to obtain powers for harm which religious practices either left in the hands of the educated Brahmans or did not bestow at all. It must be added, however, that the belief in the efficacy of repetition, so conspicuous in the modern "prayer-mills" of Thibet, is here plainly to be seen. In the Āsurī-Kalpa, as in all other Indian witchcraft practices, there is, of course, an underlying stratum of skepticism, but the

[1] Conway, Demonology and Devil-Lore, Vol I, p 272

[2] Lyall, Asiatic Studies, p 88

[3] Dorman, Origin of Primitive Superstitions, p 361

great power of the priests is tacitly recognized by the care enjoined upon one who undertakes to subdue a Brahman. The practices for obtaining blessings are confined to the latter part of the pariçista,[1] and, from their general character, seem like an extension of the original practices, perhaps for the purpose of giving additional currency or respectability to the whole; they may possibly be regarded as a further indication that the Āsurī-Kalpa, however ancient its main practices may be, is, in its present shape, comparatively modern.

At the present time in America, the interest felt in witchcraft is shown by our surprisingly large and growing literature on the subject.[2] In India the interest felt is of a different nature, but it is none the less strong. To the Hindoo the subject is a living one, and while the native literature referring to magic and superstition has always been great, at present, especially in the vernacular dialects, it is enormous, and forms the favorite reading of the people.[3] So great is its hold upon the natives that Lyall says of it:[4] "It is probable that in no other time or country has witchcraft ever been so comfortably practiced as it is now in India under British rule";[5] again, "in India everyone believes in witchcraft as a fact", and just below, "In every village of Central India they keep a hereditary servant whose profession it is to ward off impending hailstorms by incantations, by consulting the motion of water in certain pots, and by dancing about with a sword." Beside this may be placed the statement of Conway,[6] that there are 84,000 charms to produce evil made use of in Ceylon at the present time. In so far as it throws light on the past history of such practices, the work on the Āsurī-Kalpa may not have been in vain.

[1] Both MSS recognize a division of the practices into groups—*A* into two as shown by the figures (*1* and *2*), and *B* apparently into three, for it has a two (*2*) where *A* has one (*1*) and what may be a one (*1*) in the passage which it alone contains. It lacks the number at the end. The divisions of *A* have been marked in Roman numerals since it has been thought best to number the çlokas although the MSS do not do so. The practices of the second division are all of the same general nature.

[2] See Poole's Index, third edition, 1882, under the headings Witchcraft, Demonology, Magic, etc.

[3] Burnell, Sāmavidhāna-Brāhmana, I, p. xxv.

[4] Asiatic Studies, 1882, p. 96.

[5] "Of course the witch is punished when he takes to poisoning or pure swindling" (loc. cit.).

[6] Demonology and Devil-Lore, I. 274.

II.—TEXT, CRITICAL NOTES, AND EXTRACTS FROM THE SCHOLIAST

om namo rudrāya[1], *om kaṭuke kaṭukapattre*[2] *subhaga āsuri rakte*[3] *raktavāsase*[4], *atharvaṇasya duhite*[5] *'ghore 'ghorakarmakārike*[6], *amukam hana*[7] *hana daha daha paca paca mantha*[8] *mantha tāvad dana tāvat paca yāvan me vaçam ānayaḥ*[9] *svāhā.*[10] *çayyāvasthitayās*[11] *tāvaj*[12] *japed yāvat svapiti, prasthitāyā*[13] *gatim daha daha svāhā svāhā, upaviṣṭāyā bhagaṁ*[14] *daha daha svāhā svāhā, suptāyā*[15] *mano daha daha svāhā svāhā svāhā svāhā, prabuddhāyā hṛdayam daha daha svāhā svāhā svāhā svāhā svāhā*[16]

athāta āsurīkalpam[17] *upadekṣyāmo*[18] *'tharvaṇaḥ,*
nāsyās tithir[19] *na nakṣatram nopavāso vidhīyate 1.*

ghṛtādisarvadravyeṣv[20] *āsurī*[21] *çatajāpitā,*

1 ***A*** and ***S*** omit these three words. ***S*** begins *çrīganeçāya namaḥ*.—2 MSS (all three) regularly *patra*.—3 ***B*** and ***S*** omit.—4 So MSS (all three), fem. from transition stem in *-a*.—5. So MSS (all three), analog. voc., as if from stem in *-ā*. In all cases where an *a-* is elided it is written in the MSS.—6 ***B*** *-karike*, ***S*** *-kārake*, but in one passage (p. 23) *-kārini*.—7 ***B*** *hana*, ***A*** *hana 2*.—8 ***A*** omits.—9 MSS *-naya*.—10 ***S*** *amukasya matim daha daha, upaviṣṭasya subhagam* (cod. *çu-*) *daha daha, suptasya mano daha daha, prabuddhasya hṛdayam daha daha hana hana paca paca paca* (cod. *pra-*) *matha matha tāvad daha daha yāvan me vaçam āyāti hrīm hum phaṭ svāhā, iti mūlamantraḥ*. ***S*** also calls it *atharvaṇamantraḥ*.—11 ***A*** *çiṣyā-*.—12 ***B*** *-tāyāḥ etāv-*.—13. ***B*** *prachitāyāpagatim*.—14. ***B*** *magam*.—15 ***B*** omits, ***A*** *svaptāya*.—16 ***S*** **part third** *devadattasya* ['Of a certain one,' technical use] *matim daha daha, upaviṣṭāyā bhagaṁ daha daha, suptāyā mano* (cod. *marā*) *daha daha, prabuddhāyā hṛdayam* (cod. *ṛda-*) *daha daha paca hana matha* (cod. *ra atha*) *tāvad daha yāvan me* (cod. *-vakte*) *vaçam ānayo* (cod. *-ya*) *hum phaṭ svāhā*.—17 ***B*** *āsurīm*.—18 ***B*** *-deçad atharvaṇaḥ*, ***S*** *vyākhāsyāmaḥ*.—19 ***B*** *na tasyās tithi nitratram* ***S*** **part third**

çrīmāhāde (*-mahādeva*) *uvāca,*
çṛṇu vatsa mahāmantram āsurīvidhim uttamam,
na ca titha (*-thir*) *na* [*ca*] *nakṣatram na māsāunyāiva* (!) (*māsāny eva ?*) *vāsare,*
na sthānaṁ nakta (*-te ?*) *tu kāpi na vevta* (!) (*veta ?*) *ca vidhīyate 1.*

—20 ***A*** *ghṛtādidravyasarveṣv*.—21 The m a n t r a *nāsyās*, etc ?

pattradvaravaraç casyai jigīsī canupāyini,
hantukāmo hi çatrūnç ca vaçīkartum[3] *ca bhūpatīn* 2

asurī likṣṇipiṣṭāyām[4] *juhuyād ākṛtim budhaḥ,*
arkādhaṣāgnim[5] *prajvālya cittvāstrenakṛtim tu*[6] *tām* 3

pādāgrato 'ṣṭasahasram juhuyād yasya vaçy[7] *asāu,*
ghṛtāktayā strī vaçinī[8] *pālāçāgnāu dvijottamaḥ*[9] 4

guḍāktayā kṣatriyās[10] *tu vāiçyās tu dadhimiçrayā*[11],
çūdrās tu lavaṇamiçrāt[12] *rājikām piṣṭayed budhaḥ* 5

ā saptāhāt[13] *sarva ete āsurīhomato vaçāḥ,*
kaṭutāilena trisamdhyam kulocchedam karoti hi 6

çunām[14] *tu lomabhih*[15] *sārdham apasmārī tribhir dināiḥ,*

1 **A** *yatrā-* **B** *patrā-* —2 **A** *jikarṣā*, **B** *jigīṣāgamtugāmini* —3 **A** *-kurvanç ca* **S** *atha rajā, vacīkartukāmaḥ*, but elsewhere *rājavaçīkartukāmaḥ*. Cf **part third**, *rāmāvaçīkaraṇakāmaḥ* and *çatrughātanakāmaḥ* —4 **B** *āsurīm* **S** *asuryā supiṣṭayā* (cod *sursupiṣṭa-*) *pratikṛtim kṛtvārkasamidbhir agnim* (cod *-iddhih agni*) *prajvālya dakṣiṇapadarabhya* [or *-pādenā-*] (cod *-pada-*) *çastrena cittvā* (cod always *cintvā*) *ghṛtāktam juhuyāt 108 aṣṭottaraçatahomena vaçī* (cod *vaçi varçi*) [Sc *rājā bhavati*] —5 **A** *arkedhanā-*, **B** *arke-* —6 **A** *nu* —7 **A** *vatyasāu* —8. **S** *āsurīsupiṣṭapratikṛtim kṛtvā vāmapādenākramya çastrena cittvā ghṛtāktam juhuyāt 108 saptāhe siddhiḥ* (cod *sidhi*) —9 **S** *palaçasamidbhir agnim* (cod *-idhih agni*, similarly below) *prajvālyāsurim* (cod *-ri*, so regularly) *ghṛtāktam madha* (!) (*madhusahitam*?) *juhuyāt 108 homena çatyahevāra* (*-varo*?) *vaçam anayati* —10 **S** *khadirasamidbhir agnim prajvālyāsurīm madhusahitam* (cod *madha-*) *108 homena saptāhe va* (!) (*vaçī*) *bhavati* —11 **B** *madhumiçrayā* **S** *udumbarasamidbhir dadhyaktām* (cod *dardhoktām*) —12 **B** *miçritām* [Sc *pratikṛyāih*?] **S** *udumbarasamidbhir. lavanamiçram kṛtvā trisamdhyām* (*-am*) *juhuyat 108* For an enemy, **S** *asurīm kaṭukatāilāktam, limbakāṣṭe agni* (!) (*nimbakāṣṭenāgnim*) *prajvālya homayo* (*-yet*) *108 homena satpāhanna* (!) (*saptahanam*?) [or *-āhe*] *mriyate ripuh* —13 **B** *samāhat* —14 **S** *çvetakhararomā* (!) *asuri* (!) *ekīkṛtya* (*-romnāsurim eki-* or *-romāsurim cāiki-*?) *yasya nānnmām* (!) (*nāmnā*?) *juhuyād akasmād apasmārāu* (*-re*?) *gūdyate* (!) (*guhyate*?) —15 **B** (not in **A** or **S**) *çunām tu lomabhi* (*-bhir*) *atra patram lipya* (!) (*pattram lipya*?) *rhugam* (!) (*lūgam*?) *vā rājasarṣapāih samālipyātu* (*-ya tu*?) *bhūpayet* (!) (*dhū-*?),

gauregram (*-rāgram*?) *tato dadyān mriyate sāva* (*sarvah*?) *samçayah,*
abhakṣabhakṣoç cārogyam sarvarogaprayojanam

samjñātā (*-tāh*?) *pindapātān* (*-pātika*?) *japāt pāpā bhavanti hi,*
ekādaçānujaptavyam kulochedakṣato (*-cchedah kṣa-*?) *bhavet* 1 (?)

nivrttih[1] *ksīramadhvājyāir*[2] *lavaṇena tu sajvarī*[3] 7

arkāidhahsamidagnāu[4] *tu*[5] *karoti*[6] *sphotasaṁbhavam,*
tesām upaçamam[7] *vidyāt sureçvaryā*[8] *ghrtena ca* 8

aikaksīrāktayārkagnāv aksinī sphotayed[9] *dvisah,*
gatāsumānsam tasyāiva nirmālyam citibhasma[10] *ca.* 9

esām cūrṇena saṁsprsto hāsyaçīlo[11] *'bhijāyate,*
ajāksīrāktayā homāt[12] *tasya mokso*[13] *vidhīyate.* 10.

tagaraṁ kusthaṁ[14] *māṅsī ca tasyāh pattrāni cāiva hi,*
etāih çlaksṇāis tu saṁsprstah[15] *prsthatah paridhāvati.* 11

tasyāh phalāni mūlāni surabhihastimedasā,[16]
sūksmataddravyasaṁsparçād[17] *anudhāvaty acetasah.*[18] 12

vāiçyasādhane homyāç çūrṇāi (homayec chūrṇāih ?) suratibhih (?)
krtām,
catuspathe tu çūdrasya padminyotkarane yatu (yā- ?)
likhitvā nāma saṁgrhya karāgrāngulipīditam (-pīdi- ?),
çirahpīdājvarah çūlaṁ vimatih svastyasaṁgatih [svastyasaṁgatih.]
valpādyā (kal- ?) vā prayoktavyā vrahmaṇādicatustaye (brā-),
evaṁ saṁpaty abhicāraç [ca] caturṇām api darçitah.

1 MSS *nivrtih* **S** *juhuyāt pranmānayane* (!) (*pratyānayane ?*) *ksīrāktām krtvā homa (-mam ?) 108 tatah sthito bhavati* —2 **B** *çīranaghājyāir* —3. **S** *āsurīm lavaṇamiçrām juhuyāt 108 saptāhe jvarena prathānayane* (!) (*pratyā-*) *ksīrāktām juhuyāt 108 parasvastho bhavati* —4 **B** *arghedhāsa-*, **A** *arkeṅdha-* **S** *āsurīnimbapattrāni 108* (cod. *-nīva-*) —5 **B** omits —6 **A** *karovisphota-*, **B** *karute purusa sphota-*. **S** *hutvā sa visphotakāir grhyate* —7. **A** *upasa-* —8 **S** *prathānayana* (*pratyā-*) *āsurīṁ krtvā 108 svasto bhavati* —9 **B** *-tamye* **S** *āsurīm aikaksīrāktāṁ krtvā . . homayed yad asya nānmām* (!) (*nāmnā ?*) *grhṇāti tasyāksi sphotayati.* For cure, **S** *āsurīm ksīrāktām juhuyāt 108* —10. **S** *āsurīm citābhasma mahāmansam pretakam nirmālyam ekīkrtya 108* —11 **S** *mantritena camṇena* (*cūrn-*) *yasya spūnāti* (!) (*sprçati ?*) *sa unmatto bhavati* —12 **B** *hometa.*—13 **S** *āsurīm ajāksīrāktāṁ krtvā svastho bhavati* In **S** the order is "Eye-twitching," "Epilepsy," "Fever," ' Loss of sense," "Boils"—14 **A** *kusta*, **B** *nagaram kustha* —15 **S** *abhimantritena yasya spūçati* (*spr-*) *sa prsthato 'nucaro bhavati* —16 **A** *suraibhir ha-* —17. **A** *sūksmetat dra* , **B** *sūktam tadra-*.—18 **S** has,—

uçīram tagaram kustham usrām othasitghātham (!) (⏑⏑⏑) *paçcaka* (*pañcakam*),
āsurīpuspasaṁyuktam sūksmacūrnaṁ tu kārayet 108, (cod *-yet, tenācatābhi 108*)
abhimantritena (cod *mantrī-*) *yasya çati* (*sprçati*) *çavaço* (*sa vaço*) *bhavati* (*bhavet*) 14

achidrapattrāṇy asita ugrāh[1] sarṣapās tathā,
etaccūrṇat puṣpaphalam etāç cūrṇāparājayah[3] 13 I.
kusumam manahçilā priyangutagarāṇi[4] ca,
gajendramadasamyuktam[5] kim kurvanas tv akimkaram[6] 14
yaç ca[7] striyo 'bhigachanti tu vaçah padalepinah[8],
sapuṣpām[9] tām samādāyāñjanam nāgakeçaram[10] 15
anenaktābhyām[11] akṣibhyām yam[12] paçyet sa ca kimkarah
añjanam tagaram kuṣṭham[13] devījam kāṣṭham eva ca 16
mānsi ca sarvabhūtānām sāubhāgyasya tu kāraṇam[14],
tatsamidhām lakṣahomān nidhānam paçyate mahat[15] 17
sarpir[dadhi[16]]madhvaktapattrāṇām viddhaputri[17] sahasratah,
rājyam tu labhate vaçyam tatpattratrisahasratah[18] 18

1 *B* *u vam* —2 *B* puts çlokas 13–18 directly after the passage which it alone contains —3 *A* *yuvatphala ghate cāi-* *S* has instead,—
āsurīpuṣpapattrāṇi puṣpāṇi ca phalāni ca,
nāgendraphalasamyuktam sūkṣmacūrṇam tu kārayet 108,
abhimantritena yana (yasya) sprçati sa vaço bhavati (-vet) 15
—4 *B* *mriyamyu ta-* *S* has,—
manahçilā priyañguç ca tagaram nāgakeçaram,
āsurīphalasamyuktam sūkṣmacūrṇam tu kārayet 108 [aṣṭaçatāni],
abhimantritena ya(yasya) spṛti (sprçati) sa vaço bhavati (-vet) 16
—5 *B* *gajendrāsa sam-* —6 *A* *akrdvaram* —7. *A* *yasyā* —8 *A* *-lepanah*, *B* *pārasādalepalāt* —9 *B* *pumspānāmtsa-* —10 MSS *-kesaram* —11 *B* *anjanetāktām* —12 *B* *yam yam paçyet sa kimkarah* *S* *abhimantritena cakṣuṣy añjayitvā yam nirīkṣayati sa vaço bhavati* —13 *B* omits, *A* *kusta* —14 *S* has instead,—
āsuryañgapañcakenātmānam dhūpayet,
yasyāgagandham (!) (yo 'sya gandham?) jighrati (ji-) sa vaçyo bhavati 18.

It also reverses the order of the two following statements.—15. *S* has,—
dadhimadhughṛtāktām hutvāsurīm juhuyāt,
mahānidhānam labhate daçasahasrāṇi,
çatāyur vāi puruṣā (-ṣah) 20
—16 Omit on account of metre? *S* *āsurīm madhughṛtāktām hutvā labhate putram 19* —17 *A* *vṛddhapannīm* —18 *B* *tatpattratridhānam . . -trisahasratah*, repeating from çloka 17 last pāda to 18 end inclusive. It then has *sārdham . . . acetasah* (çloka 7 end of first pāda to çloka 12 end inclusive), after which it continues with çloka 19 (*suvarna-*). *S* has,—
rājyārtham madhughṛtāktām juhuyād āsurīlakṣmīm,
sa rājyam labhate 21

suvarṇasahasraprāptis[1] *tatpattrāṇāṁ tu lakṣataḥ,*
sahasrajapāc[2] *ca tadvad udake kṣīrabhakṣiṇaḥ* 19.

vāripūrṇe 'tha kalaçe[3] *palāçīpallavān kṣipet*[4],
snānād alakṣmyā[5] *mucyeta sāuvarṇakalaçe*[6] *'pi tu*[7] 20

vināyakebhyaḥ snānato dāurbhāgyāc cāiva durbhagāt[8],
pṛṣṭhataç cānudhāvanti saṁspṛṣṭā[9] *udakena tu* 21

uçīraṁ tagaraṁ kuṣṭhaṁ[10] *mustā*[11] *tatpattrasarṣapāḥ,*
cūrṇenābhihitas[12] *tūrṇam īçvaro 'pi vaço bhavet* 22.

tulasī bhūmadā devī cūrṇaspṛṣṭas[13] *tathā vaçī,*
rājabhaye[14] *sureçvarī mārjanād*[15] *dhāraṇāt tathā* 23

na[16] *syād asyādbhutaṁ kiṁ cit*[17] *na kṣudropadravas*[18] *tathā,*
nānāiçvaryaṁ[19] *nāprajatvaṁ*[20] *yasya devy āsurī gṛhe* 24

yasya devyāsurī gṛhe[21]. *II.*

ity āsurīkalpaḥ samāptaḥ[22].

1. **A** *svarṇasahasrasyāptis tu tatpuṣpāṇāṁ* **S** *suvarṇātham āsurīphalānī daçasahasraṁ hutvā suvarṇasahasraṁ labhate* — 2 **B** *sahaja-*. **S** *payobhakṣy āsurīṁ udake pralakṣiṇāṁ* (!) (*dakṣi-* ?) *dityāmukho* (!) (*pratyā-* ?) *bhūtvā daçasahasraṁ japet* —3 **A** *-laçe lokeçī-*.—4 **B** *-vāṁ kṣapet* **S** *āsurīpallavāir aṣṭaçatotī-mantrītaṁ* (!) (*aṣṭottaraçatābhimantritaṁ* ?) *saṁpūrṇaṁ kṛtvā atma* (!) (*kṛtvātmānam* ?) *snāpayeta* (*-yed* ?) *ma* (!) (*ātmānaṁ* ?) *dhūpayet* — 5 **B** *-kṣmī* **S** *alakṣmīṁ muncyati* (!) (*muñcati*), *vināye kopasvarga* (*kopasargaṁ* ?) *muñcati* —6 **A** *-phalaçe* —7 **B** *-pi va.*—8 **A** *-gān* **S** *durbhagā subhagā bhavet* —9 MSS *saṁspṛṣṭa* —10 **A** *kṛṣṭaṁ*, **B** *kuṣṭaṁ* —11 **B** *mastāṁ āsnātatpatra-* —12. **B** *-bhihatas.*—13 **B** *-ṣṭasaṁ* —14 **A** *-bhaya* —15. **B** *marjanāt, vāraṇāṁ tathā* **S** has instead, *cyartutha* (!) (*caturthaṁ* ?) *jvarādibhūtān aṣṭaçatāni japeta mārjayena* (!) (*-nena* ?) *prakṣiṇa* (*-īnam* ?) *mucyati* (*-te* ?) —16 **B** *na ca tasyadbhu-* —17 **A** *-cr na* —18. **S** has instead, *āsurīpiṣṭaṁ çatavārāṁn* (!) (*-raṁ* ?) *pariјaspya* (*-apya*) *çirasi dhāpayeta gṛhīto mucati* (*-cyate* ?), *duṣṭagṛhītānāṁ āsurīṁ homayet 108 tato mucyati* (*-te*) *kṣipram* —19. **B** *-nīçva-* —20 **B** *-pramataṁ* **S** has instead, *atha mantram prakāçayati lokānāṁ hitakāmyayā, āsurīmantraḥ sampūrṇam* (*-no*) *astu* (*'stu*) —21 MSS *gṛhe iti* —22 **A** *-taḥ.* 35

[illegible]
ıg the goddess. ***Part third*** gives a diagram of it
e duplicated. It appears that the altar-mouth was so

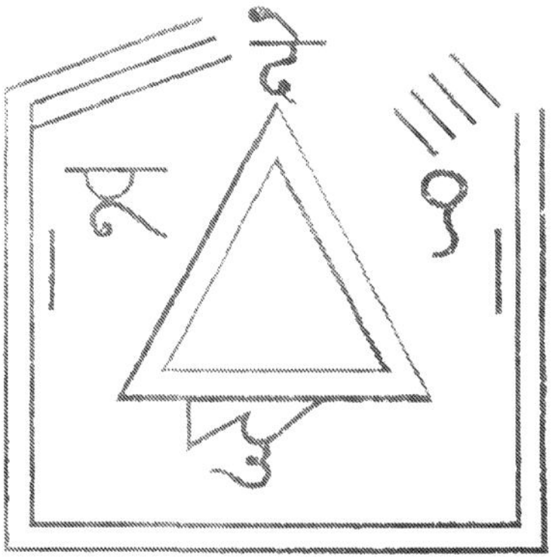

me angle pointed to the south; for the diagram has
"east," *u* for *udicī* "north," *de* probably for *dakṣiṇā*
d a figure one (*1*) which may easily be a corruption for
west." Cf. (***part first***) *puruṣahastapramāṇe* (cod.
akuṇḍe[2] *vediyonisahitaṁ sattvā* (cod. *satvā*) *dakṣiṇa-*

ing, good oblation.' Used at the end of invocations very much
m.
teral triangle has been a favorite figure in mysticism as well as
e description of the pentacle in Dictionnaire Infernal,
on, 1863, p. 518. Cf. also Cornelius Agrippa, Vol. I, p. 196 ff.,
io & duodenario cum duplici duodenarii Cabalis-
ica; also I 226 ff., De Geometricis figuris atque Cor-
virtute in magia polleant, & quae quibus elementis

kaṇṭake devīm (cod. *-vī*) *pūjayet*[1] 'Having reclined (sat down), one should worship the goddess in a three-cornered fire-pot of the size of a man's hand, with an altar-mouth having [its] point (ear) to the south' The preparation-rite includes an oblation of ghee and sugar (*ghṛtaçarkarāhoma*), garlands of the red, sweet-smelling oleander (*raktakaravīrapuṣpamālā*), an ornament (mark) of red sandal-wood (*raktacandanatilaka*), the partaking of a brahmacarya-oblation (*brahmacaryahaviṣpānaṁ bhaktvā*, cod *bhaktā*), and a lying on the ground (*bhūmiçayana*)[2] **S, part second**, adds, *dakṣiṇābhimukho nityam* 'facing the south constantly,' *kambalāsanam* 'sitting on a woolen blanket,'[3] *raktavastraparidhānam* (cod- *traṁ pari-*) 'putting on a red garment,' and *raktagandhānulepanam* 'anointing with red sandal wood powder.'[4] **S, part third**, says also, *sarvatra prāṇāyāmādiṣu* 'in all cases in the holding of the breath in worship, etc'

The address to the Āsurī-goddess, beginning the "fundamental formula," occurs in **S** several times, mostly in **part third**, with slight variations in form. In one instance it has as one of its introductory phrases, *netratrayāya namah* "obeisance to 'Three-eyes,'" and then continues, *om hrīṁ katuke*, etc Under the title *japamantrah* "whisper spell," it appears in the form, *om klīm hrīṁ çrīṁ kṣāum kṣāuṁ çrīm hrīṁ klīṁ oṁ, katupattre subhaga*

[1] **Part second** says of it *trikonakaravuyonisahitam karavuhastamātram tu kundam kāryam, onisahīta* (!) (*yonisahitam*? nardly *oni-*) *ayāta* (*athāto*?) *brāhmanadakṣinamukhavesīne* (!) (*-vāsini*?) *homa* (*-mayet*?) *karavukundanu* (!) *agna* (!) (*-de tv agnim*?) *dakṣinakaravum param* (*rā*?) *sīdhī* (*siddhih*) 'A fire-pot must be made having a triangular — altar-mouth of the size of a — hand moreover thereupon (?) one should offer an oblation (?) in the — fire pot with an altar-mouth having a situation towards the south suitable for worship (?) [having kindled] a fire moreover with a — to the south The greatest magic (success) [results]' The word *karavu* occurs nowhere else and is not at present translatable

[2] Cf **part second** *bhojanam haviṣpānam ekasuktam* (!) (*-bhuktam*?) *bhūmiçayanam brahmacaryam*, also **part third** *jitendriyah* (cod *yā*) *pūjayed āsurīm devīm* (cod *-rī devī*)

[3] For explanation see Durga Puja (*durgāpūjā*) by Pratápachandra Ghosha (*pratāpachandra ghoṣa*), note 19 p xxix

[4] It heads the preparation-rite with the words *atha padgātmantra* (*-ah*), and ends it by saying *iti damkathitam* (*-ah*) *mantram* (*-ah*) The first seems to mean, 'The going to the feet [of Rudra] text' (*pad* for *pad*) The second is a puzzle, but it probably contains some similar idea referring to the propitiation of the god

āsuri raktavāsase 'tharvanasya duhite 'ghore 'ghore svāhā, om klīm hrīm çrīm kṣāum kṣāum çrīm hrīm klīm om[1]

Following the mūlamantra, *S* gives a 'limb-placing ceremony' (*aṅganyāsa*), consisting of "obeisance" paid to the fingers in pairs, and to the two palms and backs of the hands The object of such a ceremony is said to be the mental assignment of various parts of the body to certain divinities, with accompanying gestures and prayers[2] In the present case the end in view seems to have been the propitiation of Rudra[3] Next in order comes a meditation (*dhyāna*), in which the protection of Durgā is invoked, and mention is made of some of her characteristics, among them the possession of 90,000,000 bodily forms (*durgā navakoṭimūrti-sahitā*)

> In the case of a woman lying on a couch, as long as she sleeps one should mutter 'Of her arisen the going burn, burn svāhā, svāhā, of her seated the bhaga (pudenda) burn, burn svāhā, svāhā, of her asleep the mind burn, burn svāhā, svāhā, svāhā, svāhā, of her awake the heart burn, burn svāhā, svāhā, svāhā, svāhā, svāhā[4]
>
> 1 So then we will teach the Āsurī-Kalpa of the Atharva-Veda (atharvan) For her not a 'lunar-day,' nor a 'lunar-mansion,' nor the kindling of a holy fire is decreed[5]
>
> 2 Over all material consisting of ghee, etc, the āsurī[6] is caused to be muttered[7] one hundred times, And [let there be] a

[1] For other lists of particles somewhat similar in nature, cf Durga Puja, pp 36 end f and 61 end It has been thought best to keep the anusvāra throughout, the MS uses the anunāsika sign, possibly to indicate a prolongation of the vowels by nasalization

[2] See Durga Puja, p 30 ff, and note 21, p xxxi f

[3] Cf **part third**, *tatra karāṅgulinyāsaḥ, evam rudayādi (rudrāyādāu) nyāse evam mantram (-aḥ) samam (sāma?) nyāsam (-aḥ) kartavyam (aḥ) sadhakottamāi (sādhakottamāiḥ)* 'Then the finger-placing ceremony, thus to Rudra in the beginning the nyāsa, thus the mantra, the sāman, the nyāsa is to be performed with the highest magical [rites]'

[4] ***S*, part first**, does not contain this formula

[5] 'The highest āsurī ordinance' Cf p 11, foot note 19, where a fuller but not altogether clear form of the mantra is given

[6] Probably the mantra just given, possibly the mūla-mantra

[7] Cf Laws of Manu, II 85, where the statement is made that muttering [the syllable *om*, the words *bhūr*, *bhuvah*, and *svar*, and the Sāvitrī rc (RV III 62, 10)] is ten times better than a regular sacrifice, if they are muttered so low that they cannot be understood they avail one hundred times more than a regular sacrifice, and, if they are recited mentally, one thousand times more This is possibly the starting point of the notion that muttered words and par-

> portion of this[1] consisting of leaves, etc. [Let there be] one, surely, who desires to smite [his] enemies and to render submissive kings

Owing to the uncertainty of the text,[2] it has been thought best to omit the translation of one pāda, though a provisional reading has been adopted. ***S*** has nothing corresponding to it, but reads *atha çrī āsurīmantraṁ (çryāsurīmantram) mā atharvāna ṛsih (mātharvāṇarsir) asuridevatā (āsurī-) hrīṁ bījaṁ (-m) asuri-çakti (āsurī-) nastikachaṅdah (-ndo) mama çatruksayaṁ (-yo) mārane mohane vasikarane (vaçī-) stambhane (stambh-) vini-yogah*, 'Then me possessing the divine āsurī-mantra [let] the seer of the Atharva ritual, [let] the āsurī-divinity [help ?]

ticles possess a peculiar and mysterious power which even the gods cannot escape, and by which the person understanding how to use them can control divine as well as human agencies and accomplish what he wills At the present time in India, the Brahmans consider it a sacrilege to utter the word *om* (pronounced aum as representing the trinity) aloud, and they also still attach wonderful powers to it Cf the *om mani padme hūm* of the Buddhists

S regularly gives the number of oblations as one hundred and eight and a mantra is as regularly said to be pronounced with the oblation One hundred images are mentioned by ***S*, *part second*—*sai sapatāilahomah*** (cod *pars-*) *pratimāçatah 108*—but the number 108 follows immediately, as elsewhere

[1] The āsurī-plant

[2] The reading of ***A*** is impossible as it stands, and that of ***B*** presents difficulties which can hardly be overlooked The word *jigāisa* could scarcely be anything but a secondary adjective derivative from *jigīsa*, meaning 'he who desires to conquer" (here fem), while *gamtu* or *āgamtu* might be a 3d, sing , root-aor , imv or the stem of the inf used in a compound It is difficult to see why a woman should be specified as the one desiring to conquer, and even if it were plain the rest would remain unsatisfactory The root-aor of the √*gam* is confined to the Vedas, Brāhmanas, and Sūtras (Whitney, Roots, Verb-Forms, etc) and may justly be suspected here, though the MSS seem to use some Vedic words, for example, *homa* (probably for *homam*), the √*yu* (p 98, foot-note), and *indha* (***A***, çloka 8) The infinitive stem also as part of a compound, does not here make satisfactory sense, though the form is unobjectionable The three lines taken together evidently serve as a sort of introduction to the practice, and taking the reading given in the text (as emended from the better MS), the whole may perhaps be rendered freely

> 'The āsurī-[mantra] is caused to be muttered one hundred times over all sorts of materials, such as ghee, etc , [There is to be] both a portion of the [āsurī] consisting of leaves, etc , and [there is to be] a desire to conquer without [ordinary ?] means (by magic ?), For [there is] one who both wishes to smite [his] enemies and to render submissive kings '

While this is not altogether satisfactory from a Sanskrit standpoint, it is the best that can be done at present

hrīm [There is] the core of the mantra (seed) possessing the might of āsurī, the desire to destroy, the destruction of my enemy, in the slaying, in the stupefying, in the making submissive, in the fixing like a post [this is] the practice'

Following this statement *S* has a "contemplation"[1] (*dhyāna*), in which the person should meditate (*dhyāyet*) on the bright four-sided granter of wishes (*çuklām caturbhujām*[2] *varadām*), having a hook in the hand (*an̄kuçahastām*), adorned with all ornaments (*sarvālaṁkārabhūṣitām*), seated in the padmāsana-position[3] on a serpent (*nāgopari padmāsanopaviṣṭām*), and having a gracious countenance (*prasannavadanām*) The MS then has, *iti vaçīkarane*, 'Thus [readeth it] in the making submissive' Secondly, in the fixing like a post (*stambhane*) the person is to meditate on the reddish, four-sided, fearless wish-granter (*kapilām caturbhujām abhayavaradām*), with sword in hand (*khan̄gaahastām*), having as an ornament a half-moon crest(?) (*candrārdhamāulinepathyām*?,[4] cod *caṅdārdhamāulīneprām*), etc. And thirdly, in the slaying or magical incantation for that purpose (*mārane*), he should meditate on the blue-colored, four-sided, fearless wish-granter (*nīlavarṇām*, etc), having a "red-stone" in the hand (*rudhira-*), seated on a dead-man (*mrtamānuṣopaviṣṭām*), wearing a muṇḍā-garland (*muṇḍāmālādharām*), etc The meditation contains several vocatives addressed to the goddess, for example, *kṣame*[5] "gracious one," *nāgayajñopavītini* "thou that hast a snake for sacred cord," and so on The corresponding reflection of *S*, **part third**, written in çlokas, begins. 'This is the time-triad meditation. [There is the meditation] pertaining to passion and also [that] pertaining to goodness and [that] pertaining to spiritual darkness, thereupon the highest, accompanied by all sacred rites, divine, hard to be attained accomplishment by magic [takes place],'—

atha kālatrayam dhyānam

rājasam sātvīkī (!) (*sāttvikaṁ*) *cāiva tāmasam ca tataḥ param,*
sarvakarmasamāyuktaṁ sādhanam devadurlabham I

[1] For a similar dhyāna see Durga Puja, p 34 f

[2] This word is used as an epithet of Visnu in the sense of having "four arms"

[3] A posture in religious meditation The person sits with his thighs crossed, one hand resting on the left thigh, the other held with the thumb upon his heart while his eyes are directed to the tip of his nose

[4] *Candrārdhamāuli* is an epithet of Çiva

[5] An epithet of Durgā

The three parts of this meditation treat mostly of the adornment and characteristics of a goddess The first following the passage just cited begins 'At dawn [one should meditate on the goddess[1]] shining with reddish apparel, adorned with guñja[2] and vidula (?),'[3]—

prātā (cod. *prātaiakta-*) *raktāmbarābhāsām guñjāvidumabhūṣitām* (!) (*-avidula-* ?).

It continues with similar expressions, and the third çloka reads 'The one having three eyes and having four mouths, illustrious with the murmuring proceeding from the reading of the Veda, Possessed of staves and a disk,[4] carrying a sacrifice-spoon[5] and ladle, a beautiful one,'—

trinetrāṁ ca caturvaktrāṁ vedadhvanivirājitām,
dandekamandalāiyuktāṁ (!) (*daṇḍikāmaṇḍalāir yuktāṁ* ?) *çuvahçrucadharām* (!) (*sruvasruca-* ?)[6] *çubhām. 3.*

It ends with the words *iti rājasam*, 'Thus [readeth] the [meditation] pertaining to passion.' The second begins 'At midday [one should meditate on] the goddess wearing white apparel, moreover always gracious, Having put on a white garment, carrying a white serpent,[7] Decked with garlands of mālatī[8] along with white sandal-wood ointment, etc, Having an appearance like [that of] the fruit of the ghātri,[9] made beautiful with a string of pearls in the nose,'—

[1] This meditation contains no verb, but from the meditation in *S, part first* it is evident that *dhyāyet* is to be supplied The *devīm* is expressed in the next division

[2] Abrus precatorius

[3] Calamus rotang or Calamus fasciculatus

[4] The disk is mentioned again just below in another section of the meditation There is a general tendency noticeable in both divisions of *S* to repeat certain ideas in the three parts of the meditation

[5] The constant use of these two implements together makes it probable that this is the meaning of the passage, which is very corrupt

[6] Transition stem in *-a* from *sruc* though possibly bad writing for *sruva* The sruc is a large spoon or ladle, made usually of palāça- or khadira-wood, and is used for pouring ghee on a sacrificial fire, the sruva is a small spoon used for skimming the fat from the pot into the sruc The reading *suvahsruca-* may be suspected here

[7] There are several plants called *kañcukin*, and it may possibly be one of these

[8] Jasminum grandiflorum

[9] Emblic myrobolan

çuklāmbaradharām devi (!) (*-vīm*) *madhyāhne tu sadā çivam* (!) (*-vām*),
çubhravastraparidhānam (*-nām*) *çvetakañcukidhārinī* (!) (*çvetakañcukidhārinīm* ?) 5
çubhracandanalepadyam mālatīmālāmanditām (*-pādyamāl-* ?),
ghatiphalasamakārām nāsāmāuktikaçobhitām 6

To these expressions may be added *triçūlacandrāhidharām* (cod *-hīdharā*) 'bearing a trident and a white serpent,' and *çvetavrsabhasamsthitām* 'standing by a white bull' It ends with the words *iti tāmasam* 'Thus [readeth] the [meditation] pertaining to spiritual darkness' The third division is substantially as follows 'In the afternoon moreover [he should meditate on] the goddess made beautiful with a black ornament, Having put on a black garment, decorated with an ornament (mark) of kastūrī (musk?), Adorned with three eyes in a streak of black antimony [applied to the lashes as a collyrium], Sitting down along with a bird, made illustrious with a conch-shell and a discus,[1] Possessed of a blue lotus,[2] decked with garlands of holy basil,[3] Thus at evening the goddess[4] Laksmī, in a black color, obeisance! one praises' (?),—

aparāhne (cod *-āhne*) *tu sā* (!) *tām* ?) *devi* (!) (*-vīm*) *krsnālamkāraçobhitām*,
krsnapataparidhānam (*-ām*) *kasturitilakānkitām* (!) (*kastūrītilakāñjitām* ?)
krsnakajjalarekhāyām locanatrayabhūsitām,[5]
vihange (*-hangena*) *samāsinām* (*-āsīnām*) *çankhacakravirājitām* 1[6]

[1] Cf *çankhacakragadādhara* 'holding a conch-shell, a discus, and a mace', an epithet of Visnu

[2] Nymphaea caerulea

[3] Ocimum sanctum

[4] Possibly the reading should be *rāmām devīm* 'the beautiful goddess', but there is reason to believe that it should be *ramām* Preceding the "Time-triad meditation,' there is a brief āsurī-meditation of a similar nature, introduced by the words *āsurīdhyānam ādāu ca vāidīdhyānam* (*vedi-* ?) 'The āsurī-meditation and in the beginning the altar-meditation,' in which Çrī and Laksmī are both mentioned (cod *çrīç ca te laksmi*) and the meditation of **S, part first**, referring to Durgā also mentions Laksmī The tendency of the MS to repeat has been mentioned

[5] *trilocanī* is an epithet of Durgā, *trilocana*, of Çiva It is probable that the *netratraya* used in a form of the mūlamantra (p 17) refers to the latter

[6] The numbering of the MS has been followed

nīlotpalasamāyuktām tulasīmālāmaṇḍitām,
eva (-vaṁ ?) sāya (-yaṁ ?) ramā (-māṁ ?) devi (-vīṁ) kṛṣṇavarṇe namo (-maḥ ?) stute. 2

The next passage is almost hopelessly corrupt. It contains enough syllables for more than three çlokas, has the figure four (4) at the end, and seems to emphasize some of the items already mentioned.[1] It concludes with the words *ity adi (-dāv ?) āsurī-trikāladhyānam* 'Thus in the beginning [of the rite (?) readeth] the āsurī time-triad meditation' Further references to the goddess follow, among them, *mahādevi (-devy ?) aghorakarma-kāriṇī*[2] (-ṇi ?) "great goddess non-terrific deed-performer." The whole ends as follows 'And also [thou who dost grant] much compassion [and] who dost bestow many a success, The meditation of Brahma, Visnu and Çiva, deliver the three worlds, O mother[3] Thus precisely [readeth] the supreme meditation. O āsurī, supreme mistress, [Thou art] the giver of success to the magical [rites] producing enjoyment and deliverance. Thus in the beginning [readeth it] in the āsurī-meditation,'—

aneka (-kaṁ ?) cāiva kāruṇyāṁ (-yam ?) anekasiddhidāyini, (-iṁ dā- ?),
brahmaviṣṇuharadhyānaṁ trāhi trāilokyam ambike. 3

ity eva paramadhyānam āsuri parameçvari,
sādhakānāṁ siddhidātā bhuktimuktiphalapradā. 4

ity ādi (ādāv ?) āsurīdhyāne

The significance of these references to the goddess āsurī will be discussed below. It appears from the references to the three parts of the day that the oblations were made at the periods named, and the three parts of the meditation, in the order given, were used with them, i. e the one referring to rajas was used in the morning, that referring to tamas at noon, and the one refer-

[1] The passage begins with the words *sāttvikaṁ puvāhe*, which should probably be emended to *iti sāttvikam pūrvāhne*, for the conclusion to the third part of the meditation is lacking in the MS, and the words *madhyāhne* and *aparāhne* follow in the two succeeding lines The reference to the trisaṁdhyam becomes clear only on the supposition that *sāttvikam* ends the third division, and that the rest of the passage is supplementary to the whole

[2] The passage is too corrupt to determine whether the words should be voc or acc , but they are probably voc. Cf the passage cited just below, also p 11, foot-note 6

[3] Commonly used of Pārvatī, wife of Çiva, i e. Durgā

ring to sattva in the afternoon.[1] The number of oblations has been mentioned above, and it will be again considered below in another connection.

3 The wise man should offer as an oblation a mixture of ghee and fine āsuri-meal [in the form of] an image, Having kindled a fire of arka-wood fuel, having chopped the image, moreover, with a weapon.

4 He [becomes] submissive before whose feet [a person] offers eight thousand oblations. A woman [is made] submissive by [an image of āsuri-meal] anointed with ghee. Brahmans in a fire of palāça-wood.

5 Ksatriyas, moreover, by [an image] anointed with sugar, but Vaiçyas by [one] mixed with curds, Çudras, furthermore, by [those][2] mixed with salt: the wise man should make meal of black mustard.

6 As a result of an oblation of āsuri [extending] up to the seventh day,[3] all these [are made] submissive.

The practice in full[4] seems to have been as follows. The wizard first ground āsurī[5] into meal, with which he made an image, symbolizing the person whom he desired to overcome.[6] He used kindlings (samidhs)[7] of arka-wood for Rājās and

[1] It is to be observed that the corresponding meditation in *S*, ***part first***, is also divided into three minor reflections. No time is mentioned with the divisions in that place, but it is probable that the same rule was observed as that laid down in ***part third***. It also appears from the former, that each reflection was regarded as instrumental in accomplishing some particular part of the complete process of subjugation or destruction.

[2] The change to the plu. masc. seems at the first glance to be for the sake of the metre, but since *çūdras lavanamiçrayā* makes even a better pāda than the one in the text, it may be inferred that a different word was purposely implied in the case of Çūdras. As a matter of fact the word most appropriate to them is masc. Cf. çloka 5 and foot-note.

[3] Cf. p. 12, notes 8, 10, and 12 end; also p. 13, note 3, and p. 27.

[4] See çlokas 3, 4, and 5, and foot notes.

[5] Probably the leaves as well as the seeds. See translation of çloka 2.

[6] Cf. ***part third*** (beginning of the rite used to subdue a Brahman), *purva-brahmatimām* (*pūrvabrahmapratimām*?) *krtvā* 'having made the former image of a Brahman,' i. e. as before.

[7] The samidhs used in offering oblation were small sticks of wood about a span (9 in.) long and about as thick as a man's thumb. Cf. Colebrooke, Asiatic Researches, VII 233. The usual number is seven, but the Grhyasamgraha-Pariçista of Gobhilaputra gives nine and their names (I 28 f.),—

ity etāh samidho nava,
viçirnā vidalā hrasvā vakrā stūlā krçā dvidhā, 28
krmidastā ca dīrghā ca varjanīyāh prayatnatah.

women, palāça-wood for Brahmans, khadira-wood for Ksatriyas, udumbara-wood for Vāiçyas and Çūdras, and nimba[1]-wood for foes Having chopped up the image with a sword, he finally offered it as an oblation, adding ghee for a king or woman, ghee [and honey[2]?] for a Brahman, sugar for princes, curds for third caste persons, salt for fourth caste persons, and pungent mustard oil for foes.[3] It is to be observed that in the case of a king the person was to advance with the right foot, in that of a woman, with the left. This is doubtless to be put with the similar Hindoo notion that the throbbing of the right eye or arm is lucky for a man and unlucky for a woman, while with the left eye or arm the case is reversed

S*, *part third, while much fuller in its details than the other two sections, adds little of importance or interest. A few points in which it differs from them may be mentioned, for example, in the rite used for ensnaring a king it has *ravikāṣṭhena prajvālya* 'having kindled [a fire] with a stick of ravi[4]-wood', it also pre-

Dr Bloomfield, in his edition, thus translates "dies sind die neun samidhs (Zündhölzer) Ein zerbrochenes, ein gespaltenes, eins das kurzer (als eine Spanne) ist, ein krummes, eins das dicker (als ein Daumen) ist, eins das zwei Zweige hat, ein von Wurmern zerfressenes, und eins das langer (als eine Spanne) ist, sind nach Kraften zu vermeiden" The most complete description of them, however, is to be found in the grhya-sūtras

[1] In the order named these trees are the Calotropis gigantea, the Butea frondosa, the Acacia catechu, the Ficus glomerata, and the Azadirachta indica Some idea of the Hindoo view in regard to these woods may be obtained from the Āitareya-Brāhmana, II 1, The Erection of the Sacrifice-post (*yūpa*), and their appropriateness may be inferred from the Laws of Manu, II 45, where it is stated that the Brahman's staff should be of vilva- (Ægle marmelos) or palāça-wood, the Ksatriya's, of vata (Ficus indica) or khadira-wood, and the Vāiçya's, of pilu- (Careya arbora or Salvadora persica) or udumbara-wood Çūdras are not dvijas "twice-born," and so do not come under the rule For *nimba*, ***part third*** uses *picumanda*, which is only another name for the same wood and verifies the emendation (p 12, foot-note 12 end)

[2] See p 12, foot-note 9

[3] The use of an image is treated of in the Introduction above Kāuç Sū, adhyāya 6, contains further material of a similar sort See Kāuc 35, 28, 17, 54, and 49, 22

[4] Böhtlingk, Lex. V, 172, cites ravi as the Calotropis gigantea which makes it identical with arka In this sense it seems to have been known heretofore to the lexicographers only

This article was in type before I had access to the index to Böhtlingk's lexicon, which also contains the word aparājaya and perhaps others It has not been in my power to carefully consult that work for all the new or doubtful words in these MSS

scribes in this connection the "whisper-spell" (p 17 above) in that for ensnaring a woman[1] it has the heading *rāmāvaçīkaraṇa-kāmaḥ* and refers to the two fundamental formulas[2] (*mūlamantrāu*) under the ensnaring of a Brahman it prescribes white sandal wood, a white wreath, and a white garment with other ornaments (*çvetacandanasaṁyuktam çvetamālā- . . . çvetavastra-samanvitam*), the oblation must also be performed with especial care (*prayatnena homayet*) and in preparing it use is made of balls of Guggula[3] gum (*guggulāir guṭikāḥ*—cod. *gugulāi guṭikā—kṛtvā*), black mustard seeds (*rājasarṣapāḥ*), leaves of the betel-plant (*nāgavallīdalāir hutāiḥ*), and other vegetable products, such as fruits and flowers,[4] finally, under the subjugation of a Çudra, it mentions also the Cāṇḍālas. A few passages from the same division may be cited with reference to the number of oblations and the time for performing them In the rite used against women 'Afterward the muttering is to be performed, moreover, one hundred and eight times by (of) men,'—

paçcāj japaṁ tu kartavyam aṣṭottaraçatam nṛṇām

'Having muttered the fundamental formula in the mouth and [having performed] one hundred and eight [rites], The girl wastes away in (of) her middle [parts], thereupon the girl is likely to become submissive,'—

mūlamantre (-tram) mukhe japtvāṣṭottaraçatāni ca,
daçyate madyānām yoṣā tato yoṣā bhaved vaçā.

[1] Under this heading four different uses are given with considerable minuteness of detail The words employed to designate a woman are, *rāmā* "beautiful woman," *yoṣā* "girl, young woman," and (once only) *strī* "woman, wife" The words used to signify her subjection are, *vaçagā* "obedient" (second use), *vaçī* "submissive" (third use), and *vaçyagā* "subdued" (fourth use) (This last word is also used of a Vāiçya and of a Çūdra) In the first use where *strī* occurs, it is difficult to say what the word is It appears that the practice was used in some instances as a philter, and there is even reason to believe that this may have been its most common use Cf Virg Ec VIII 64 ff, Hor Sat I, VIII 23 ff, and Epod V, Lucian Dial Mer IV 4 and 5, Ovid Met VII 224 ff, and Heroid VI 91, and see çlokas 14 and 15, and p 8, foot-note 2

[2] It will be remembered that two formulas were given for a woman Under the preliminary rites in **part third** the plu is used (*mūlamantrāiç ca*)

[3] Bdellium or the exudation of the Amyris agallochum

[4] From the statements here made, and another passage (p 12, foot-note 9) which says that by oblation 'a certain high number consisting of hundreds' (*çatyahevara*) leads a Brahman to one's will, it may be inferred that the eight thousand oblations of the text (p 12) have special reference to Brahmans

In the rite for a Vāiçya 'Having done this (kindled the fire and performed the other preliminary rites), at the three periods of the day, he should burn the prepared ā s u r ī [made into an image] With one hundred and eight [rites] so long should he perform the muttering at the three periods [morning, noon, and afternoon],'—

evam dinatrayam krtvādhyāktām (-aktām ?) āsurīm dahet,
aṣṭottaraçatāis tāvat trikālam japam ācaret. 3

'One should perform with pains the muttering during one month uninterruptedly,'—

japam kuryāt prayatnena māsam ekam nirantaram

Under this heading also (first ç l o k a) the dark fortnight, i e from full to new moon (*krṣṇapakṣe*) is specified as a time for performing the rite In respect to a Kṣatriya, it is said that he should be subdued in the course of twelve days (*dvādaçāir vāsarāih*). Finally, regarding a foe, it says 'At the eight periods (watches) of the day having done honor with the m a n t r a he goes against [his] foe, On the seventh day the completion of the foe-slaying becomes fixed,'—

param pratyeti mantrena pūjayitvā dināṣṭakam,
saptāhe ripughātasya nidhanam bhavati dhruvam (cod *dhivam*). 3

Most of the references agree in fixing the completion of the ensnaring on the seventh day One hundred and eight oblations performed in six days amounts to just eighteen per day, and these performed at the t r i s a m d h y a m would make six in the morning, six at noon, and the same in the afternoon, which was evidently the plan followed as a rule.

With pungent mustard oil [in the oblation][1] at the three periods of the day, surely one makes a split in the family

7 With the hairs of a dog,[2] moreover, [a person is] afflicted with

[1] It is probable that ā s u r ī was to be used in this and all of the following prescriptions, though it is omitted in many of them

[2] The passage which is found only in ***B*** at this point is very corrupt, yields no connected sense and contains nothing of importance It is probably an interpolation Its general meaning seems to be about as follows

'Having then, moreover, smeared a leaf with the hairs of a dog, or having well smeared with mustard seeds (!) he should fumigate the l i ṅ g a (perfume it with incense)

He should then give a measure (?) of white mustard drink all doubt vanishes (dies) And there is health in eating and in fasting [it is] the practice in all diseases epilepsy during three days[1] The stopping [of this is brought about] by milk, honey, and ghee [in the oblation] [By performing the rite] with salt, however, he [becomes] afflicted with fever'

8 In a fire of arka[3]-wood samidhs, furthermore, one establishes a source of boils Of these he should understand the cure (stopping) with the help of sureçvarī and with ghee

The word *sureçvarī*, which occurs in one other passage below (p 33), is thus defined by the PETERS LEX Bez der Durgā der Lakshmī . der Rādhā . der himmlischen Gañgā It here means evidently āsurī[4] (probably both plant and divinity) The use of this word for *āsurī*, combined with the fact that various words found in the āsurī-meditation (p 20 f) are or may be used of Durgā, makes a strong presumptive argument that āsurī was regarded as a form of Durgā. *sureçvarī*, however, may be used of Lakṣmī, who is spoken of in the same connection, and who appears again below It will also be observed

Surely the well known ones who live by alms (?) [Brahmans] become bad as a result of muttering It is to be muttered eleven times in succession The split in the family may become destroyed (he is likely to become injured by a split in the family ?)

In the subjugation of a third caste person he should offer as an oblation (?) [an image] made with powdered suratis (?) (surabhis "nutmegs" ?) In the overcoming (doing up) of a Çūdra, moreover, let [the person] go (?) with a lotus-plant (*padminī*) to a place where four ways meet

Having written the name, having seized [it] pressed by the finger (?), [there arises] headache, fever, [and] colic Disagreement is a non-meeting with prosperity, a non-meeting with prosperity

Or the ādyā of the kalpa (?) [is] to be used in a quaternion of Brahmans, etc thus in their coming together, the magic practice of the four even is made manifest'

The word *ādyā* is a puzzle It is an epithet of Durgā, but can hardly be used in that sense here If for *ādya* (neu), it may possibly refer to the mūla-mantra as the beginning of the kalpa It does not seem likely that the MS reading *valpādyā* is a new word

The scenting the liñga with incense may possibly be a love-charm Cf, however, Herod I 198, ὁσάκις δ' ἂν μιχθῇ γυναικὶ τῇ ἑωυτοῦ ἀνὴρ Βαβυλώνιος, περὶ θυμίημα καταγιζόμενον ἵζει, ἑτέρωθι δὲ ἡ γυνὴ τὠυτὸ ποιέει

[1] *S* 'Having tied up (made one) the āsurī [in the form of an image ?] with a hair from a white ass, he with whose name he may make oblation is suddenly afflicted with (hidden in ?) epilepsy'

[2] āsurī and milk are used in making the one hundred and eight oblations for his restoration to health

[3] *S* has simply āsurī and nimba leaves

[4] *S* 'Having made āsurī, 108, he becomes well (in his own condition)' *ghṛtāktām* is probably omitted

that a large part of the dhyānas consists of "stolen thunder,"[1] a fact not to be wondered at, since the people who used these rites were hardly capable of originating any ideas themselves, and would naturally borrow any that might seem suitable. In the same way they would refer to deities, especially evil ones, who might be regarded as likely to give success. A mixture of direct reference to āsurī, and allusions to these other divinities, is therefore to be expected, and clear conceptions are hardly to be looked for, since confusion of the two sets of ideas is almost inevitable with an untrained mind, and it is to be seriously doubted whether those who practiced the rites had any really definite idea as to the exact meaning of their 'prayers.' The confusion of divinities would probably only make the spell appear all the more potent because of the mystery[2] which it created; for the mysterious is an essential element of all magic.

> 9. In a fire of arka-wood, with [āsurī] anointed with arka-plant and milk, [a person] may cause the two eyes of [his] foe to twitch (burst).

S adds a clause which is not altogether clear. The √*grabh* regularly takes the acc., and emending to *nāma*, the meaning is, 'When he mentions his name.' If emended to the ins.,[3] which seems more likely from the MS. reading, the use must be a technical one in some such sense as: 'When he grasps [the image] along with the name,' i. e. having the name attached to it.[4]

[1] Cf. references to the Durgā Pujā, foot-notes, pp. 18 and 20.

[2] That the capacity of the Hindoo mind for the mysterious is not small can be seen from a stanza in the RV. (X. 54, 3), in which Indra appears as the begetter of his own parents:

> *ká u nú te mahimanaḥ samasyāsmát pū́rva ṛ́ṣayó 'ntam āpuḥ,*
> *yán mātáram ca pitáram ca sākám ájanayathās tanvàḥ svā́yāḥ.* 3.

Grassmann thus translates: "Gab je es Sänger, welche vor uns lebten, die deiner ganzen Grösse Ziel erreichten? Der du zugleich den Vater und die Mutter aus deinem eignen Leibe du erzeugt hast." After this, some obscurity in the thought and a slight confusion of divinities may be pardonable in such a document as the Āsurī-Kalpa, in which the object in view is not so much the sense as the use of potent words and particles to accomplish a result by magic.

[3] Cf. p. 12, foot-note 14, which favors the emendation.

[4] Cf. pp. 9 and 27, foot-note 2. **Part third** begins the practice with the words *atha netranāçanam ravikāṣṭhe kṛte home*: 'Then the eye-destruction. Oblation having been made on a stick of ravi-wood.' It prescribes āsurī, arka-plant, and salt in the oblation, and says: 'And the seventh day having arrived (been obtained) he becomes deprived of his eye,'—

> *saptame vāsare prāpte çcakṣuhīnaç (!) cakṣurhī-) ca jāyate.* 3.

The flesh of a dead man, his remains of course, and ashes from a funeral pile[1]

10 He who [is] touched with the meal [made] of these becomes possessed of a ridiculous character[2] Deliverance from this is produced as a result of an oblation with [āsurī] anointed with goat's milk

11 Tagara, kuṣṭha, and mānsi[3] plants and also certainly leaves of this [āsurī] He who [is] touched with these [ground] fine, moreover, runs about behind [one's] back[4]

12 Fruits and roots of this [āsurī] with the fragrant fat of an elephant From contact with fine material of these[5] [a person] runs after those devoid of sense

It adds 'Then the cure (causing to cease) Having made an oblation of āsurī anointed (?) with cow's milk, with fires of ravi-wood as a result of his own oblation (*maha*) he becomes well (goes to the being in his own condition), the eye-disease should disappear (become vanished),'—

atha çāntāu (*-tiḥ* ?)
godugdhenāsuriptupta (!) (*-rīm liptām* ?) *hutvā ravihutāçanāiḥ,*
svamahāt svasthatām yāti netrarunī mihitā bhavet

Part first has 'āsurī anointed with milk' The similarity of the means used in producing and curing the evils is noteworthy as an evidence of the popular notion in India that he who can cure disease must also be able to produce it and vice versa

[1] ***S*** 'Having united āsurī, ashes from a funeral pile [and] human flesh, the remains of a dead [man]' ***Part third*** adds fire chopped meat, the hair of a Cāndāla, and some other things not yet clear (*ullakamayāiḥ*),—

āsurīm ca citābhasma janaḥ piçitam samyute,
cāndālakeçasamyuktam ullakamayāiḥ saha (*sahitam*),
mrtanumālyasamyuktam ṣadir (*-im* ?) *ekatra kārayet* 2

(*ṣadi* is probably a fem derivative from *ṣad* in the sense of "sixness," a collection of six The person unites the six items mentioned) It puts this rite under those to be employed against an enemy, ending the whole with the words *iti çatrukṣayavivaranam* 'Thus [readeth] the detailed account of the destruction of an enemy'

[2] ***S*** 'out of his senses' It adds that the mantra is to be pronounced over the meal

[3] Tagara is Tabernaemontana coronaria, also a powder made from it, kuṣṭha is a plant used for the cure of takman (fever?), the Costos speciosus or arabicus, mānsī may be jatāmānsī (Nardostachys jatamansi), kakkolī, or mānsacchandā The MSS seem to require a plant called kuṣṭhamānsī No such plant is mentioned elsewhere so far as known The omission of the anusvāra is easily explained, and it appears in çloka 22 ***S*** reads, *nagara kuṣṭa te upatnī mānsi*

[4] ***S*** 'becomes a servant (attendant) behind [his] back'

[5] ***S*** mentions five plants besides āsurī flowers tagara, kuṣṭha, uçīra (fragrant root of Andropogon muricatus), usrā (Anthericum tube-

13 Uninjured leaves [of āsurī] the dark uçīra-root, likewise mustard seeds From the meal of these the former result[1] [is produced] and also by these invincibleness [is obtained][2]

According to *A* this marks the close of the first division of the practices, all of which thus far have been for the purpose of producing ill, curing the same, or getting the mastery of some one In all of them the materials have been ground into meal, to be used either in making an image of the intended victim or to be applied to him in person Those that follow have already been discussed above

14 Flowers [of āsurī ?], realgar, and millet and tagara plants, With the juice from the temples of a huge rutting elephant,[3]

[4]

15 And the women who approach [become] submissive to (servants of) the one anointing their feet Having taken this [āsurī] in bloom, añjana,[5] [and] nāgakeçara-plant

rosum), and some other plant which is not clear. The *tgh* may possibly stand for *jh* (p 13, foot-note 18), in which case an emendation to *jhātā* (Jasminum auriculatum) might be suspected A correct pāda can then easily be made, though there is no MS authority for it, by omitting the doubtful word *othasi usram jhātām tu pañcakam* It prescribes the mantra, and says, 'He whom he touches becomes submissive'

[1] Probably the running after those devoid of sense

[2] *S* says, 'He should make into fine meal, moreover, āsurī-flowers and leaves, and flowers and fruits, along with fruit of the nāgendra (betel ?) He becomes submissive whom he touches with [this meal] consecrated by mantras muttered over it' The use of the mantra, or muttered spell, seems to be an essential element in all these practices

[3] The reading *-medasa-* 'fat (of a huge elephant),' may be suspected here possibly, though the evident nature of the compound favors the MS reading

[4] The two MS readings of this pāda are neither of them entirely satisfactory The MSS agree save in the two middle syllables of the last two feet *S* gives no help It reads 'He should make into fine meal, moreover, realgar, and millet, tagara [and] nāgakeçara (Mesua roxburghii) plants, along with āsurī-fruit [He should mutter the spell] one hundred and eight [times] (one hundred and eight [mantras should he mutter] ?) He whom he touches with [this meal] consecrated by the mantra muttered over it becomes submissive' From the connection it appears that the pāda must refer to or contain instructions for the person using the philter *B*'s reading would mean then

'[Let him be] preparing [the mixture], however, (*kim* *tu*) without help (in the manner [of one] having no servant)'

The idea may possibly be that the power of the charm would be impaired or diverted if another had anything to do with it The *akrd varam* of *A* seems to mean 'not acting the suitor,' or something similar Cf p 14, foot-note 6

[5] An eye salve or ointment made from Amomum xanthorrhiza or antimony, used as a cosmetic

16 He whom[1] [a person] looks at with [his] eyes anointed with this [compound becomes his] servant Añjana, tagara, kustha and devījakāstha[2] precisely,

17 And mānsī plants [are] a cause of good fortune, moreover, to all creatures From an oblation of one hundred thousand of the samidhs of this [āsurī] great treasure is beheld[3]

18 From one thousand leaves [of āsurī] anointed with ghee, curds[4] (?), and honey [in the oblation, a person becomes] possessed of grown-up sons One obtains, moreover, a submissive kingdom from three thousand leaves of this, [āsurī, offered as an oblation]

S says, 'For the sake of a kingdom one should make an oblation of āsurīlaksmī anointed with honey and ghee, he obtains the kingdom' Laksmī is used as a name for several propitious plants, evidently by a sort of personification, and its use here as an extension of the name for black mustard is significant because it is also used in the āsurī meditations above

19 The obtaining of one thousand gold pieces [comes] from one hundred thousand leaves[5] of this [āsurī, offered as an oblation], And likewise one thousand mutterings of him who partakes of milk over water[6]

20 Then in a vessel filled with water let him strew palāçī twigs He is likely to be freed from ill-luck[8] as a result of an ablution, in a golden vessel, however

[1] *B* 'whoever he looks at,' a better reading in some respects, but *S* supports *A* It also adds the usual muttering of spells over the salve

[2] Probably kāsthа-dāru (Pinus deodora), called also deva-dāru Here called "goddess born" *S* has a different statement 'He should perfume himself with the smoke of five parts of āsurī [flowers, leaves, etc], he who smells the scent of it becomes submissive'

[3] *S* 'Having offered an oblation of āsurī anointed with curds, honey, and ghee, he should make an oblation, he obtains great treasure, ten thousand [oblations should he make] A man [will reach] the age of one hundred years you know [if he does this]'

[4] *S* and the metre both favor the omission of this word

[5] *S* 'ten thousand āsurī fruits, having offered as an oblation'

[6] *S* 'Having partaken of milk over āsurī and water [and] having taken a position facing the south (?), he should mutter ten thousand times

[7] A species of climbing plant, called pattiavallī, parnavallī, and palāçikā *S* 'With āsurī twigs having made full [a vessel] consecrated by one hundred and eight spells muttered over it, he should bathe himself, he should perfume himself (?) with incense'

[8] *S* 'He sets aside ill-luck, in good breeding he puts away the disposition to (onset of) anger' (?) The reading *vināge kopa-* is suspiciously like *vināyakebhyah*, but other similar cases occur

21 [A person is likely to be released], as a result of an ablution, from obstacles and also from unfortunate ill-luck And touched by the water, moreover, they run about behind [them] [1]

22 Uçīra, tagara, kustha, mustā,[2] mustard seeds, and leaves of this [āsurī] When quickly touched with meal [made of these] even a lord should become submissive

23 Tulasī, bhūmadā, [and?] devī[3] Touched with the meal [made of these?] likewise [a person becomes] submissive In case of fear of a Rājā, [let] sureçvarī be used From purification with it, likewise the carrying [it with one] [4]

24 No portentous occurrence is likely to be his, likewise no small misfortune [He is] neither devoid of power nor destitute of children in whose house the divine āsurī is, in whose house the divine āsurī is [5]

Thus endeth the Āsurī-Kalpa

[1] ***S*** 'An ill-favored woman should become well-favored' The ill luck seems to be especially a husband's dislike, and the last clause may mean, therefore, that the husbands become very attentive

[2] A species of grass (Cyperus rotundus) ***S*** omits.

[3] This line is not clear tulasī is the Holy Basil, devī may be one of several plants, Sanseviera roxburghiana Medicago esculenta, Trigonella corniculata, etc, and bhūmadā "earth giver," may be a plant or simply an epithet of one If a plant, it is probably āsurī (cf *varadā* used in the meditations) Two other meanings are possible 'Holy basil, the earth giving goddess,' and 'Holy basil [and] the earth-giving goddess [āsurī]' ***S*** has a different statement 'Fourthly, with respect to [evils] such as (consisting of) fever, etc, one should mutter [the spell] one hundred and eight times By means of a purification, destruction is averted' For *prakṣīṇa* cf Peters Lex, *prakṣīṇam idam devadattasya* "Dies ist der Ort wo D umgekommen ist' It might be rendered Here the death (destruction) of D [took place]'

[4] ***S*** has, 'Having muttered [the spell] one hundred times (?) he should put āsurī-meal on his head He who has been seized is released . For those who have been overpowered by sin (?) he should make an oblation of āsurī one hundred and eight times, thereupon [the person] is at once released'

[5] In place of this statement ***S*** has 'Thereupon he causes the text to become clear by the good-will of men Let the āsurī text be completed' It adds the usual ending

'The Āsurī-Kalpa [is] concluded'

Lightning Source UK Ltd.
Milton Keynes UK
UKHW020827270223
417728UK00007B/661

9 781016 237932